# Success @ 60+

## 7 swift steps to your Superlife

Bridget Postlethwaite

and

Jane Aireton

# Acknowledgements

Thank you to all those without whom this book would not have been possible, Carole Ann Rice for her Forward, Chandler Bolt for his book *Book Launch,* Didi Hill for her ode, Eileen Barnett for her advice, Emma Farrarons for calming me down with her mindfulness colouring book, Jenny Moseley for her advice, Jake Woodnutt and Judith Vonberg for photography, Judith Vonberg for being our Editor, Lois Fitzgerald for her advice, Marjorie Oakden for her advice, Matt at Candescent Press for formatting! Matthew Herivel for the cover, Mike Aireton for bearing with me and supporting, Rachel Abbott for her advice and inspiration, Rosemary James for her advice, Ruth Hughes for fashion advice, Sarah Weldon for her inspiration, Dr Susan Wilson MBE for her inspiration, Tissie Roberts for her advice, Tara Darby and Robin Arzon for their inspiration and all those who have inspired and encouraged us along the way.

Dedicated to all those Superlifers whose lives are
beginning to change…

'When I let go of what I am, I become what I might be.'
Lau Tzu

# Contents

# Bridget and Jane

Bridget and I are passionate about empowering women to push their boundaries and achieve their potential; blowing mediocrity out of the water and living life to the full. In Success @ 60+ we are putting the spotlight on the over 60s from the perspectives of our different experiences.

We have both lived on the Channel Island of Alderney for many years. Bridget is a widow who cared for her husband whilst running an estate agency and is now taking her 'gap year', selling her house and setting off into the unknown to the amusement of her four children and seven grandchildren.

I am a nurse who has looked after my older family members for the last fifteen years and now am setting sail on a new tack, which involves downsizing, writing and travelling. I have a husband, two sons and four grandchildren and have always wanted to write and inspire women.

# Foreword by Carole Ann Rice, Life Coach and Author

Really there are no excuses. There has never been a better time to truly be who you have always thought you could be. Age may indeed wither us around the edges but vitality for life, a desire to learn and a commitment to reclaim life on your terms is something we can achieve at any time if we have our health and the intention to do so.

No need to slide into elasticated-waisted beige invisibility, no need to timidly shuffle into other people's expectations and no need to live by someone else's rules. Now is the time. It takes the human brain 90 days to create a new neural pathway, which means adopting a new habit, dropping an old one or learning something entirely new.

You now have the freedom to really get to know yourself; what makes you tick, what really drives you, gives you pleasure and what you want to do without servicing other people's needs. Whether it's taking up yoga, Pilates or meditation, starting an online business, training to be a life coach or mastering the world's fairways, now you can simply please yourself.

Banish limiting beliefs that say 'I'm too old/ underconfident/past it' and dare to be curious, try things on, have a go and in the spirit of 'well, what have I got to lose except my boredom'. Dare to dream, live well and live large and may this book provide the wheres, hows and inspirational gunpowder you need to score all your goals in the second half.

**Carole Ann Rice** –Life Coach, Author and Happy Monday columnist for the Daily Express.

# Success @ 60+

## 7 swift steps to your Superlife
## Blow mediocrity out of the water!

Including your personal
journal/workbook at the end
of each chapter

# Day 1

# Introduction

# Day 1

## Introduction

If you have picked up this book I would expect you to be 60+ and looking for something to add value to your life. If so, you have come to the right place.

This book was written initially for women but we have been surprised at the number of men who have felt it to be of value to them. So, in a twist of the usual disclaimer, wherever we have used the terms women, she and her, please assume men, he and him, if applicable!

Seven steps fit neatly into a week. This time next week you could feel a very different person and in a month you could LOOK very different. There is nothing like feeling trapped, unfulfilled and useless to age you and nothing like a positive goal to reverse the effect. Enthusiastic happiness is a great recipe for a facelift. The secret is not in skin care, but in being more alive – something that is free, achievable and depends on YOU alone.

Each of the seven steps consists of a series of 'mini steps', which will gradually lead to radical change.

'The man who moves a mountain begins by carrying away small stones.' (Confucius)

Listening to Wimbledon whilst I write, it occurs to me that to win the match the players must concentrate on each point. Each toehold you secure brings you one step nearer to winning. To concentrate on the outcome at the beginning dilutes the process.

We are all on different rungs of the ladder, but these rungs are all leading to the same place. Success will be personal to YOU. In the eyes of the world success is fame and money but to you it may be something completely different; pushing your personal boundaries to achieve something you never dreamed possible.

Find the sections of this book that apply to you and use them to change the status quo.

I started out with a very clear agenda but as soon as I started putting pen to paper, or more accurately, engaging fingertips with keys, the subject, slippery as an eel, wriggled from my grasp and started growing in ways I could not have envisaged. The project took on a life of its own and flew higher and higher, challenging me to follow.

My passion was to engage with women of 60+ and share with them my new-found vigour and enthusiasm to push the boundaries and to experience a new, exciting and fulfilling side of life. A relatively simple task, I thought. Not so. The results have been fascinating and have led me on a personal adventure, which I now have the privilege of sharing with you.

My original title was 'Superlife @ 60'. Having mapped this out, I changed the title to 'Success @ 60+' as many of the women I spoke to were in their seventies and eighties. From these conversations the book took off. I started looking at the meaning of success and how it relates to happiness.

We all know that happiness and success dance around each other with complicated rhythms and intricate steps. Weaving in and out of this complex relationship is pleasure. How does this fit into the picture? In my mind, happiness is the overarching principle whereas success is much more specific and pleasure may derive from success. To enter this cycle of happiness, success and pleasure you need to find a grain of success so the seed of happiness can germinate.

I shall never forget an extreme example of this. For many years I worked as a medical matron in a girls' boarding school. One senior pupil was struggling to achieve the A grades expected of her. Her parents had assumed that if they spent enough money, they could buy her good grades, but instead this girl gradually became sicker and sicker. No doctor could find the cause and she eventually ended up on a life support machine. This was a girl who could find no success anywhere. Intellectually she was clearly not up to the challenge, nor was she particularly good-looking or coordinated. She did not fit the restrictive mould into which she had been forced by her parents and she opted out of life completely.

On the other side of the coin you can, for example, be very successful financially but desperately unhappy in your private life. Happiness and success are not automatic bedfellows.

So how can you find a goal that will make you happy or do you need to be happy before you find your goal? Clearly success on its own is not enough.

I can promise you one thing. Read this book and some of the women whose stories I tell will inspire you on your most difficult days. Start implementing some changes in yourself and you will soon have your own story to tell your grandchildren. Don't live through others, but inspire them with your life and begin TODAY. It can be terrifying but the rewards are immense. If you don't change the process you will never change the outcome.

As women we find it extraordinarily easy to send ourselves on guilt trips. How worthy in the grand scheme of things is it to pursue our own success and happiness? According to Aristotle, 'Happiness is the meaning and the purpose of life, the whole aim and end of human existence.' Who am I to argue with Aristotle?

It is certainly true that happy people are more productive, more helpful and more creative than those who are unhappy. Those words can put an end to all feelings of guilt once and for all. Being happy will energise you, which in turn will lead to more successful activities that make you happy, which in turn boosts your self-esteem. What is the opposite of a vicious cycle? A happiness/ success cycle of course. Go for it!

As Gandhi said, 'Be the change you wish to see in the world.'

'We don't see the world as it is. We see the world the way we are. We see it through our own lens.' (Kaufman) Powerful stuff!

To break into the happiness/success cycle today we can start by sowing the seeds of happiness. There is a wonderful man in the US called Barry Neil Kaufman, who runs courses on happiness amongst other things at The Option Institute. 'Happiness is a choice along with misery, anger, sadness,' he teaches. 'These states of mind are optional not inevitable.' His books, *Happiness Is a Choice* and *Power Dialogues*,[1] document the process he originated and teaches.

Kaufman had a son Raun who was autistic and destined for a life in an institution. He refused to see this as a tragedy unlike all the professionals around him. He and his wife

Samahria saw Raun instead as a precious gift and worked out a system to bring him back into their world. As a result of their success with Raun, the Son-Rise Program® was devised and children with autism all over the world have benefited. Raun attended Brown University, an Ivy League college, and now lectures at the Option Institute®/Autism Treatment Center of America® and worldwide; a graphic example of taking the apparently disastrous and turning it into brilliant success. He recently published a book entitled *Autism Breakthrough*.[2]

If success is reaching a defined goal, then happiness can be realising that you are able to reach that goal. If you are reading this book, it is perhaps because you feel that you have not reached your potential and that you have more to give.

Have you defined your goal?

If a vague desire for success in a particular area of your life arises out of a sense of precious time on this earth running out before you have left your mark, this book will get you going on the right track and help you find direction if you need it.

If you know where you are going, it will provide the encouragement and tools you need.

The reward is the happiness of fulfilling your goal and enjoying a sense of excitement and adventure along the way.

We have had fun writing this and hope you will feel our passion as you read on. We visualise you: fired with enthusiasm, breaking through the barriers that once held you captive.

Initially I used the word 'freedom' in the subtitle and I still think that it is an awesome result of success. Freedom is defined as 'the power of self-determination and boldness of conception and execution', strong words which will apply to you in a week's time. I was also fascinated to discover that 'Freedom' is an app that locks you away from the Internet so you can be more productive! The same aim as this book in fact.

It is remarkable that the years between sixty and eighty are largely uncharted territory. We are an invisible group; we don't even have a name or if we do, it isn't brilliant. The terms Silver Surfers, the Third Age or pensioners just don't do it for me. Our collective title needs to reflect a far more uplifting dynamic. People talk about babies, infants, children, adolescents, young adults, adults, middle age (forty to sixty) and then…old age. I think the word Superlifers is much more energetic and positive. This book is about challenging your expectations, assumptions and reactions. Maybe the term Superlifers will speed you on to make these exciting changes!

We live in a society that idolises youth and tends to throw the rest on the scrap heap. When I looked online for a photograph to put on the cover of this book showing a dynamic Superlifer, I couldn't find one anywhere. All other ages were represented. Fashion also tends to leave us stranded so I am tackling that later in the book.

60+ is a sort of no man's land when it could be a goldmine. Personally, I am not going to stand for that. Browsing websites for the over sixties, I notice we are often portrayed as overweight and prosaic, and addressed in a condescending manner by younger people. Not only can we stand on our own two feet (ironically, only one of mine is functional at present but that is a temporary problem), but we can also show those youngsters a thing or two.

Sister Madonna Buder, or the Iron Nun as she is known, started running at forty-eight and at eighty-two she entered the record books at an Ironman Triathlon in Canada where she became the oldest woman on the planet to complete such a competition. In total she has completed four hundred triathlons and forty-five Ironman triathlons. For those who are not aware of the distances involved in an Ironman competition, it consists of a 2.4-mile swim, 112-mile cycle ride and a 26.2-mile run. She has now opened up several new age groups in these competitions. The Iron Nun feels she is a positive example of active aging, squeezing in her training between her day-to-day duties. She runs to church and to the prison where she ministers and cycles forty miles to the lake where she trains. Her book *The Grace to Race* tells her extraordinary story.[3]

As a result of the invisible years between middle and old age, and as part of our rebellion against convention,

Bridget and I have set out to explore the potential of this powerful group and to inspire you to make the most of these golden years. Follow us on our journey to discover you can do more than you ever imagined.

As a member of the Superlifers, if you start doing something vaguely exciting or different, people begin saying 'Oh I wish I could do that' or 'you are brave' or, more commonly, 'You're bonkers', as though your course of action is inappropriate. Don't let people's opinions of you define your sense of self-worth.

Lois, one of our local radio presenters, says 'You should listen to yourself and allow yourself to believe that whatever you feel is valid and important and that, whichever path you take, you are perfectly entitled to take it. Your own opinion has real value and finding that out was what did it for me. After many years of self-doubt I accidentally found myself at the age of seventy doing a job which I love and which has real value. How did I get there? By being willing to try something new and scary because it was something that I felt needed to be done. It really was accidental; I heard about a new project, wrote an email to encourage the people making it happen, and voila! I became part of the team and I love it.'

Bridget and I have been celebrating our sixties in different ways. Bridget is selling her house in Alderney and is setting off on an unknown adventure across the world, her 'Superlife gap year'. I am downsizing on the island, aiming to build a tiny home on a trailer on the mainland so I can follow my dreams and we are writing this book to encourage women; a lifelong ambition.

Didi Hill writes…an ode to my friend Jane:

Now that we're 60 plus
What's all the fuss?
To make sure we have fun
We'll make sure it's for everyone.
Do the things we've always wanted to do
Like going on a zip wire
Or having a tattoo…
Do it now do it on a whim
Whether it's a she or a him.
Say I've done it.
That's for sure.
You never know………….. you might go back for
more!

My friend Maggie advised, 'If you have a tattoo done,
ensure it is on a wrinkle-free part of your anatomy!'

By the time you are in your sixties it is commonly
supposed that you are wisely conventional and have all the
answers – after all, you have lived long enough! Not so.
Some are wise at seventeen; some never find wisdom. The
crucial factor here is change.

Throughout our lives we are changing and adapting;
having children, grandchildren, a career or two, retiring.
On top of this are health issues, relationship issues and
financial issues. Our reactions spring from our experience,
which builds over the years. Nothing stands still; we are
either moving forwards or slipping backwards. Many
inspirational books are written by young people who see

the light and then follow it or older people who have written about the experiences of their youth.

Our take is different. We are starting on a new adventure with lived-in bodies, some of which may be falling apart at the seams, and minds that may boast a spectacular baggage collection. Our experiences of life may, in some cases, have jaded us and leeched out our joie de vivre. Some of us may have put our lives on hold at some point for some reason and are struggling to catch up. Some of us may never have realised just what we are capable of.

If every morning you would like to wake up with excitement and enthusiasm and stretch into a day full of purposeful achievement, whether it is making money, creating a quilt, moving house or flying on a zip wire over Eden, then read on and blossom into the person you were designed to be.

If you are still caught in the carer's/career trap, use your mind and start to free yourself. If I had had this book when I was barely coping in a sea of exhaustion looking after the oldies, it would have made a huge difference. It would have been like a lifebelt to a drowning man.

Action is the result of thought and thoughts can move mountains; they can flow unimpeded by circumstance and are completely confidential until you choose to give voice to them. If life's difficulties have made you too tired to think, we will do it for you, but to succeed you need to put the plan into action and to seek out the freedom to do so.

Bridget is at the beginning of her Superlife; I am well on the way through. We are very different personalities in different situations but we have both broken out, each in our own way, defying convention and throwing caution to the winds. We both love life and we want you to love it as well.

When you too break free and liberate that amazing human spirit inside you, the sky is the limit. Happiness from being fulfilled and doing more than you ever dreamt you could will change you forever. We will remind you of ways to increase your energy, your earning power and your confidence, to face the future with excitement and curiosity.

Because of the positive power of curiosity, Michelangelo was designing St Peter's Basilica in his seventies and eighties. The phrase 'ancora imparo' is often attributed to him: 'I am still learning.'

These changes can happen in an instant, or over a year, light bulb moments when fear, worry and anxiety will evaporate. Whether you learn a new skill or start a new business, the foundations are the same. If you can identify the bars that confine you, discover who you are and decide where you want to go, there is nothing stopping you except yourself.

But, but, but, I hear you say – butts are there to be sat on and that's all there is to it! If you have a full time caring/career role, then start planning and get your route map ready.

Bridget and I are living proof that life after sixty can be fantastic, as are all those people we have quoted. Once this book is published our hope is that you will be writing in with your own stories so we can write the sequel! More living proof of Superlifers' success.

Send them to success60plus@gmail.com

Start a progress diary right away to keep track of what is going on in your life and in which to do the exercises. There is a workbook section at the end of each chapter if you would like to use it. This is a fast track course so you have no excuse to drop out.

At the end of 2014 we both tried a 365-day 'achieve anything' course but after two months we couldn't sustain the momentum. Life comes in waves like the ocean so pick a patch between two breakers and jump on your board to catch the next wave of opportunity as it comes along.

As you go through this book write down where you are right now, who you really are, what you really want, where you are going and how you are going to get there. You will be amazed how quickly things start slotting into place. Woolly thinking is out, positive action is in…as from tomorrow.

'Just Do It'

# Workbook Day 1

What have I learned today?

........................................................................................

........................................................................................

........................................................................................

........................................................................................

........................................................................................

........................................................................................

........................................................................................

........................................................................................

........................................................................................

........................................................................................

........................................................................................

........................................................................................

........................................................................................

........................................................................................

........................................................................................

## Day 2

# Make happiness a priority in your life and success will follow

# Day 2

# Make happiness a priority in your life and success will follow

There are two points that require clarification.

In the context of this book you may not feel you are particularly UNhappy, but merely dissatisfied. Please read on, it still applies to you.

Advertisers intimate that buying their product will bring you happiness. It is important to differentiate between pleasure and happiness. Their products may bring you pleasure, but happiness comes from within. Pleasure is temporary; happiness can be permanent if you invite it into your world.

When I planned 'Superlife @ 60' this chapter didn't exist. As soon as I changed the title to 'Success @ 60+', happiness poked its head over the parapet and demanded to be included – most inconvenient as it disturbed the whole plan for the book. Now I regard it as the most important part of the whole exercise.

As human beings, we all have an invisible electrical system, which can be picked up, for example, on a heart monitor trace. When someone with negative energy comes into your space you can cut the air with a knife. When someone comes into your space with strong positive energy you can feel the atmosphere lifting. On a global scale this has a big effect.

I like to think of a pair of the old-fashioned weighing scales with two pans. Every time you generate positive energy it goes into one pan and every time you generate negative energy it goes into the other. This analogy is a brilliant incentive for loading up the positive side of our planet. Bridget describes this as being an optimist or a pessimist, but I am not sure that is deep enough – however, she is the eternal optimist!

Life-affirming change at 60+ will happen much faster if you are 'Happy' with a capital H. You can change that situation here and now. It doesn't cost anything; it doesn't take any time; it doesn't need any energy. You simply need to rewire your responses and reset your defaults.

As the Dalai Lama says, 'Happiness is not something ready made. It comes from your own actions.'[4]

At the Option Institute International Learning & Training Center in Massachusetts (U.S.A), Barry Neil Kaufman teaches a wonderful system to make happiness a reality in your life. If you believe that unhappiness is forced on you from outside, then there is nothing you can do about it. You are stuck. You are a victim. If you believe you can create your own happiness the whole picture changes.

Kaufman gives you the tools and the map to self-trust and empowerment, so if you are looking for a practical course go to www.option.org.

Rosemary, into her third decade as a Superlifer, was recently run over by a car and has refused to let her significant injuries prevent her from enjoying life to the full, including a trip to Australia. She sums up her attitude like this: 'through success and disaster keep a smile on your face.'

Unhappiness almost always comes from a belief that there is something inherently wrong with you. You are 60+. What have you done with your life? If you haven't been the success you wanted to be so far, what hope is there now?

Track back to your beliefs about yourself. Jot down a quick list. Next to each one add where you believe they came from. If you don't know, just guess. Maybe they were instilled by your parents or your teachers? Once you identify and remove the negative beliefs about yourself, your behaviours begin to change.

We all collect evidence to support our beliefs. How about evidence from the positive side of the fence? That is where the important evidence lies. If one of your parents were jealous of you they may have implanted strong feelings that you were a waste of space. Until you root those out, no matter what you do, nothing will seem like success. How many adults are still trying to impress their long-dead parents? Take stock of the evidence but beware the damaging self-fulfilling prophecy, 'I am no good so I will fail.' If you believe that, you will fail regardless of your track record to date!

The way we see things actually changes the way we experience them. If you see something as a tragedy, you work with it as a tragedy; if you see it as an opportunity, you make an opportunity of it. Life is what you make it.

Here are your happiness actions for today:

### ONE. Start accepting yourself without judgments.

'Self-criticism and self-doubt may be normal (usual) but not natural (as in "a necessary part of the human condition"),' says Kaufman. Judgments and self-criticism will not get you anywhere. They need to be turfed out along with blame. Your new approach starts today.

Write yourself an honest character reference. As you do it, do not judge yourself. You are a learner; you don't need to be judged.

*Bridget comments ... When I was ten, my teachers tried an experiment one term where we each had to write our own school report.*

*I wrote, 'I was a bit noisy, quite untidy and not very good' – accurate but damning. The teacher annotated the report with 'full of enthusiasm, gets carried away with a task and has a lively mind'. Wow, I thought, is that really me?*

*I had forgotten that report until some forty years later when my mother showed it to me. But at fifty I appreciated that noisy, slightly wild child – and also the value of looking twice at our own 'characterisations'.*

*Do that personal character reference – and then revisit it with a deeper understanding of the underlying emotions. You may surprise yourself. In any case, give yourself a hug for being you.*

**TWO. Start liking yourself a bit more.**

Put pen to paper again to answer these:

Why do you enjoy being you?

What do you feel satisfied with yourself for?

What makes the real you smile?

What past acts or achievements do you like to remember?

If you find this hard, just have a go – you only need a few sentences, not an essay!


**THREE. Act as if you are happy today, even if you are not.**

This is not a false front, glossing over the things that are breaking your heart or making you disillusioned with life. It is turning what has already happened into something positive.

Keep your inner eye open and turn your negative thoughts into positive ones.

You may find that you have accidental negatives you are not aware of. Your brain thinks in pictures not words and not all words translate into pictures; for example, 'I do not want to be fat.' The picture here is 'fat'; there is no picture for the word 'not'. Where your thoughts lead, your energies and power will follow. Unwittingly, you are now concentrating your energies on FAT. 'I want to be slim' sends thought power in the direction of SLIM.

To change something effectively and quickly you identify the goal, direct the thought power and take the appropriate action.

1. Set happiness as your goal and think of yourself as happy. Practise feeling happy and light.

2. Research (which is what you are doing now) needs to be followed by development for change to occur. So get off your butt.

If you have time to read this book you have time to practise happiness. As a woman you can multitask, so whilst you are driving/doing chores/dropping off to sleep you can be developing the happiness pattern.

Watch out, there are pitfalls inherent in change. People get into the habit of relating to you in a certain way and can be quite put out and even hurtful to you if you start developing a different pattern of responses. You might expect everyone to be really pleased that you are changing but believe me there will be some who aren't. They may, for example, be using you to boost their feeling of self worth; they need to feel that they are better than you in some way. There will be others who seem to be breaking your happiness pattern by annoying you.

In that case, the broken record technique works wonders. Just select a positive phrase. If it is your nearest and dearest, it could be 'I love you' (although you may not feel that way at that moment!), or, if it's someone in the office, 'I really like your outfit.' As they are going on and on and on, don't answer their questions or accusations, just keep repeating the phrase. For a while they will continue, but in the end they have to stop and ask, 'What did you say?' Now their train of thought has been broken and their thoughts are heading in a slightly different direction. The next step is to take the time to draw breath and be positive. You may need to do this several times.

If they ask 'Why did you say that?', you can reply 'because it is true'.

In some cases, it is best not to enter into a dialogue at all if you can help it. Some people are bottomless pits of need. Nothing you say will change things so get away quickly before they suck you dry. Remember, you never have to justify yourself. As women we have diplomas in apologising and justification.

'I am so sorry that I can't help you with the coffee morning. I have to pick up the grandchildren, get the cat to the vet and clean the house.'

In fact, you may be heartily relieved that you can't do the coffee morning – you may personally hate such functions. Why do they have these events? To provide a meeting place for the lonely and raise funds for charity. You may not be lonely and coffee mornings may not be your forte. If you are busy, just say so. If your success goal is doing coffee mornings, and giving all the pleasure that entails, that is perfectly fine but still steer clear of apologies and justification.

Instead, say 'I can't make it, but here is a contribution to the charity'. They are happy, you are happy and no apologising has gone on. Apologising and feeling guilty waste a great deal of the energy that you are going to need for your success.

Unless you have a cast iron reason to apologise DO NOT DO IT.

Happiness is a choice that you can make right now. You are in control. No one on earth can make you feel unhappy (or dissatisfied) unless you allow them to.

You are the gatekeeper and the guardian of your soul. Remember how precious this is and how important it is to cherish it and surround it with love and happiness. Not only will you benefit but your change in attitude will begin to make things happen around you. You are moving from personal happiness to an awesome chain reaction of happiness.

> *Bridget comments ... Having lived most of his life on a tiny island where everyone chats and smiles all the time, my youngest son found it disconcerting that people in England did not do this. We devised a game whereby, when walking into town, we would each nominate someone walking towards us for the other person to smile at. You got a point if they smiled back! We soon dropped the points system – it was a joy and brought us happiness to see someone else, often somewhat surprised but clearly pleased, smiling back at us. You might like to try it!*

You can now see a brilliant way to put a smile on the face of the world. You can 'pay forward' the benefit of your new-found happiness.

Bridget and I may have helped you on the happiness path and you have paid us back by buying our book. You can, however, still pay our gift forward by inspiring or supporting other inspirational women, young or old. In that way you are starting a chain reaction, which will begin to make the world a better place.

Here is a happiness action you can do right now.

Find a woman who you think is awesome and make contact; linking up with inspirational women brings an energy all of its own. You may not be able to support them financially but your encouragement alone means a great deal when you are struggling to achieve a goal, as you well know!

Here are mine:

1. Sarah Weldon rowing an ocean a year to inspire the next generation: www.oceansproject.com

2. Tara Darby making an inspirational film, *Run It Out*, about a remarkable young woman, Robin Arzon,[5] who ran five marathons in five days in a desert in Utah for Multiple Sclerosis research: www.runitout.co.uk

'Robin is unique because she has ripped up the rule book. She has completely blown the idea of distance out of the water. She refuses to conform and is brave enough to follow her instincts and not let obstacles stand in her way. She has suffered and overcome some extreme situations and has refused to let them destroy her life. In fact she has drawn strength from every hardship she has experienced.' (From 'Like the Wind Magazine')[6]

> *Bridget says ... Sometimes a woman you find inspirational will be stunned by your admiration. Some of the women I am completely amazed by and in awe of are overcome with surprise when I tell them how much I admire what they are doing and why. Please don't forget to tell other people when you think they are great or that what they are doing is exceptional. It may make a world of difference to them on that day – or forever – just to hear it.*

Using this method you are multiplying your gift exponentially and THAT is what happiness is all about...

# Workbook Day 2

| My beliefs about myself | …came from |
| --- | --- |
| | |

My character reference

..............................................................................................

..............................................................................................

..............................................................................................

..............................................................................................

..............................................................................................

..............................................................................................

..............................................................................................

..............................................................................................

Why do I enjoy being me?

..............................................................................................

..............................................................................................

..............................................................................................

..............................................................................................

..............................................................................................

..............................................................................................

..............................................................................................

..............................................................................................

What do I feel satisfied with myself for?

..............................................................................

..............................................................................

..............................................................................

..............................................................................

..............................................................................

..............................................................................

..............................................................................

..............................................................................

What makes the real me smile?

..............................................................................

..............................................................................

..............................................................................

..............................................................................

..............................................................................

..............................................................................

..............................................................................

..............................................................................

What past acts or achievements do I like to remember?

........................................................................................

........................................................................................

........................................................................................

........................................................................................

........................................................................................

My inspirational women are ...

........................................................................................

........................................................................................

........................................................................................

I am going to support them by ...

........................................................................................

........................................................................................

........................................................................................

........................................................................................

........................................................................................

........................................................................................

# Day 3

# Who are you?

# Day 3

## Who are you?

'I was once afraid of people saying, "Who does she think she is?" Now I have the courage to say, "This is who I am."' (Oprah Winfrey)[7]

You are now off the starting blocks.

We want YOUR story, so please keep a diary as you go so that you can keep track, see your progress and we can be amazed.

Send it to: success60plus@gmail.com

You are a product of your parents' genes and influenced by the environment in which you have lived your life so now is the time to re-set your default settings. WHO exactly are YOU?

This is the foundation of the change process from a sixty-something to a Superlifer. If you are less than honest here, the whole journey will grind to a halt.

As Gloria Steinem says, 'The truth will set you free but first it will piss you off!'[8] You need to start where you are, not where you would like to be.

Many women spend so much time caring for family members that they have forgotten who they are, or have changed out of all recognition since they last looked. Others think they are the same as they were twenty years ago, but solutions you used then may fail you now. Life depends on change and renewal. You physically change, your circumstances change, your priorities change, your reactions change.

In the toolkit of life there are two hammers, the blame hammer and the hammer of determination. The blame hammer has no place in your new life so throw it out here and now. The responsibility to move forward comes from you and you alone.

> *Bridget comments … Years ago my eldest son was going through a particularly tough time. I said to him I'd always been told that the tough times were 'character-forming'. He replied sadly that he felt he'd been formed enough.*

*Yes, things will almost certainly have been difficult in the past and this will have ranged from just difficult to unimaginably horrendous for some. But you are here now, you are not defined by your past, but the past has helped to develop the backbone of your future.*

You are now in the driving seat. You have seen how you can change any belief in the twinkling of an eye by identifying it, reviewing its history, deciding whether or not it is useful to you and dealing with it.

Maya Angelou sums it up succinctly: 'I can be changed by what happens to me but I refuse to be reduced by it.'[9]

We all collect evidence for any position we assume so choose your stance and start assembling the evidence to support it.

Saying 'I am hopeless with money' probably means you are frightened of looking at your bank statement and keep spending without checking the balance. WHY? Where did this come from? Did you get into debt and are in denial or was this feeling instilled by your parents? Do you feel you do not deserve to have money? You need to grasp the nettle and check your balance. Remember that whatever prompted your feeling is no longer valid. Make a budget using a calculator or Excel spreadsheet and get to grips with the situation. Money is merely a tool but a cunning tool; if you don't control money, money will control you!

*Bridget comments … If this is your bête noir, do the maths, find out your position and look ahead to how this can change as you gain control of your life.*

The great thing about figures is that they are totally logical and unequivocal. You can't negotiate the answer to a sum and it doesn't look worse if your day is going badly; it is what it is, whatever the weather. The stock market is, of course, an entirely different proposition but we won't go into that!

The hammer of determination will drive in the nails to secure the framework of your new decisions on which the fabric of your new life will hang.

So who are you?

Are you a glass half-full person or a glass half-empty person? A glass half-full person will find this book easier than a glass half-empty person; however the latter, as we have seen, can consciously change their view. If you are naturally likely to see the downside in a situation, keep an eye on your thoughts and as soon as a negative one appears change it to a positive.

You may class yourself as a realist but your current thought patterns have got you where you are now. If that is where you want to be, you don't need this book. If you don't like where you are now or want to improve things, start to change your thought patterns.

Albert Einstein's definition of insanity was 'doing the same thing over and over and expecting different results'.

You might say, 'Shall I start a business?' and then think, 'Oh I couldn't do that; I am too old, I tried once and it failed.'

What did you learn? Would you like to start over, or did you not enjoy the experience?

If you didn't enjoy being an entrepreneur, then don't do it. If you enjoyed the process but not the outcome, learn from your mistakes and try again.

> *Bridget comments ... Is there someone else out there doing something to which you could add value through experience? You might find it interesting and rewarding to make the offer – they may be struggling in ways you can't imagine.*

If you are not making mistakes you are not taking enough risks! Those who sneer from the sidelines are, by definition, those who have never sailed away from the shore. Walk alongside those who wish to empower you and add value to your life. Who are these people? Write down their names and their talents.

## What sort of personality are you?

You have already done a brief exercise in the introduction. Now is the time to flesh it out.

You need two columns into which to divide the words you select:

| 1. How I am | 2. How I would like to be |
| --- | --- |
|  |  |

*Active, Adventurous, Ambitious, Attentive, Authentic, Bold, Calm, Caring, Compassionate, Creative, Curious, Eclectic, Emotional, Empathetic, Energetic, Expressive, Extroverted, Flexible, Friendly, Generous, Gentle, Grateful, Happy, Honest, Humorous, Idealistic, Imaginative, Independent, Intelligent, Introverted, Kind, Loving, Mysterious, Open-minded, Opinionated, Passionate, Playful, Positive, Practical, Quick-witted, Quiet, Rebellious, Reliable, Resilient, Respectful, Romantic, Sensible, Sensitive, Sensual, Shy, Sociable, Spiritual, Spontaneous, Strong, Thoughtful, Unique, Wacky, Warm*

It is interesting to see how many sides to your personality there are. What a fascinating person you turn out to be when you examine your persona in detail. If you know you want to get out of your rut but are not sure where to go, this will offer a few ideas which will develop as you probe deeper into who you are.

By now you will have some idea which parts of your personality you would like to change. Select the three attributes that most define you from the list above and think about how they affect the life decisions you make and how they fit into the success plan you are forming.

**Now for your character.**

This time, jot down your character traits in two columns:

| 1. My character | 2. As I would like to be |
|---|---|
|  |  |

*Beauty Seeker, Bohemian, Change Agent, Connector, Critic, Dreamer, Entertainer, Explorer, Feminist, Flirt, Flower Child, Free Spirit, Fun Lover, Giver, Harmony Lover, Individualist, Lifelong Learner, Listener, Lover of Life, Master of Reinvention (useful!), Nitpicker, Observer, Optimist, Peacemaker, Perfectionist, Pessimist, Philanthropist, Philosopher, Protector, Realist, Risk Taker, Sceptic, Spiritual Seeker, Survivor, Talker, Teacher, Thinker, Truth Teller, Warrior, Wild Child, Young at Heart*

**How about your lifestyle?**

Again, make two columns:

| 1. Where I am now | 2. Where I would like to be |
|---|---|
|  |  |

*Animal Lover, Artist, Bargain Hunter, Bookworm, Cat Lover, Dog Lover, Downsizer, Early Bird, Employed, Entrepreneur, Family Person, Fashionista, Gypsy, Health Nut, Hippie, Homemaker, Internet Junkie, Nature Lover, Night Owl, Nomad, Pet Owner, Political Junkie, Retired, Rural Lover, Self-employed, Shopaholic, Social Butterfly, Urban Explorer, Volunteer*

## What position do you hold within your family?

Breadwinner, Carer, Daughter, Divorced, Grandparent, Heart of the Family, Married, Parent, Solo Flyer, Step-parent, Widowed

## How does your family affect who you are?

Are you caring for them?

The caring role is tough and can involve a great deal of emotional blackmail, often unintended but nevertheless damaging. This role can be a drain not only emotionally but also financially. The difficulty is that you never know how long it will continue.

Breaks for you may be so difficult to arrange that it often seems too much effort to do so. It is vital that you can escape in your head and plan your future.

A supportive partner is a bonus.

Your partner or your children may be holding you back and that is a tough call but you only have one life and it is very precious, so consider your options very carefully.

You have a tendency to emulate or become like the half-dozen people who are closest to you so choose wisely!

What is great is that you are reading this book and getting closer to Bridget and me – and we are two positive people for a start. If you can find a friend to do this with you, you're halfway there. 'Sixty and Me' is a great website for finding more people if necessary.

Write a list of your friends and relatives with whom you are in close contact. Put them in two columns: positive and negative. Use the saw in your toolkit to excise the dead wood amongst your friends. You can't afford to hang onto those who are dragging you down if you are trying to fly. If there is someone close to you who is bleeding you dry emotionally and you can't get away from him or her, you need to distance yourself virtually.

My friend Annie taught me a wonderful trick the other day. Put your left hand palm down over your heart pressing gently on your skin and your right hand palm facing outwards about half a metre away from your body at the same height. The left hand reflects your energy back into your body and your right hand deflects negative energies away from you. If you are feeling vulnerable and depleted this simple exercise can be a huge comfort. Try it now.

Are you a career woman who has retired and needs a new direction in her life? I know a wonderful doctor who, when she retired, became a sculptor and launched classes for the elderly. She has taken her hobby and turned it into a passion for depicting life in the raw in three dimensions. Having added value to others all her life she has continued doing the same in a different direction.

Another huge and inspirational success story, stemming from a complete change of direction, is that of Rachel Abbott, a British author of psychological thrillers. She spent most of her working life as the Managing Director of an interactive media company, developing software and websites for the education market, but in the run-up to becoming a Superlifer she became a self-publisher. Combined, her first four novels have sold over 1.5 million copies and they have all been bestsellers on Amazon's Kindle store. Everyday life ceases to matter once you become immersed in one of her psychological thrillers! A lovely and generous lady, she has encouraged so many others to fulfil their dreams.

Are you the breadwinner, meaning that the success you crave will change your financial position?

This puts extra pressure on your decisions, particularly now that pensions are not what they used to be. One of the reasons I wrote this book was because when I said to a friend of mine, 'I need to create an income stream reasonably quickly,' she replied, 'Well at your age that WILL be difficult.'

This is a common perception of people over sixty; they are past it, over the hill, washed up. Rubbish! We have got an abundance to offer. If people are so blinkered they can't see through our wrinkles that is their loss. If you can't find employment, start something yourself. There are plenty of ideas out there. For example, see Lydia Quinn's book, *21 Online Business Ideas You Can Start Tomorrow with No Money.*[10]

## How is your health?

This will be tackled later in the book, but here are a few pointers to think about in the meantime.

To make changes you need energy, which implies good health.

Many of our health problems are stress-related so making changes to relieve that stress, which in itself is often caused by feeling trapped, will be good on its own. Does your dermatitis clear up when you go on holiday? Relieve the stress and you will often relieve the problem.

Diet is the basis of good health, so is it time you looked more closely at what you are eating?

What tablets are you taking? Do you really need them? What are their side effects?

Are you looking after your weight? Do you want to use up your precious energy reserves lugging around those extra pounds or doing something more fun?

How are your energy levels?

Once you have reviewed your profile you are ready to move on, but don't take yourself too seriously!

'I realise that humour is not for everyone. It's only for people who want to have fun, enjoy life and feel alive.' (Anne Wilson Schaef)[11]

# Workbook Day 3

| How I am | How I would like to be |
|---|---|
| | |

| My character | As I would like to be |
| --- | --- |
| | |

| Where I am now | Where I would like to be |
| --- | --- |
| | |

Friends and relatives

| +ve | -ve |
| --- | --- |
| Bridget | |
| Jane | |

# Day 4

# Where are you?

# Day 4

## Where are you?

Having built up a picture of who you are, the next step is to define where you are at this moment in time. Unless you take the time to do this, the next stage of deciding 'where you want to go' will be fuzzy.

Luckily this process is quick and easy and builds on the work you have already done.

**Personality**

How are your relationships? (good/bad/indifferent)
Do you wish to change them?
Does your next move (mental/physical) involve other people?

Do you have a partner?
Have you had a partner?
Are you looking for a partner?


## Health

Are you comfortable with your weight?
Are you suffering from a limiting illness?
Do you have physical limitations?
Are you happy with your current level of exercise to keep you fit?


## Finances

Are your finances in good shape?

Check your chosen road to success. If the driving force for change is financial and if your progress benefits others in any way, there will be no speed limit on that road.

We all know the expression 'paying back'. Try 'paying forwards' (not necessarily financially) and you will be amazed at the results. If someone wants to pay you back for something, say instead 'Pay it forward to someone else'. Carry out a random act of kindness today and watch miracles happen.

Eight-year-old Myles Eckert found a twenty-dollar bill. He decided to pay it forward to a soldier he knew with the following note. 'Dear Soldier – my dad was a soldier. He's in heaven now. I found this $20 in the parking lot when we got here. We like to pay it forward in my family. It's your lucky day! Thank you for your service. Myles Eckert.' Lt. Col. Dailey was overcome by the thoughtfulness of a little boy who has had to make the ultimate sacrifice – the lifelong absence of his father. CBS got word of Myles' kind gesture, and the story that followed was shared via email and social media more than half a million times. Little did Myles know that his 'pay it forward' gesture would ultimately touch millions of lives.[12] The power of that twenty dollars was and continues to be profound when shared with love.

## Your Home

How do you feel about your home, your cave, your base? A firm foundation where you feel comfortable is a great start to creating a success. However, this is not always necessary or possible.

From 1953 to her death in 1981 a silver-haired lady walked more than 25,000 miles across America. Her t-shirt bore the words 'PEACE PILGRIM'.[13] She vowed to 'remain a wanderer until mankind has learned the way of peace, walking until given shelter and fasting until given food'. She walked without a cent in her pocket, not affiliated to any organisation. She touched the hearts and minds of thousands of Americans as she walked and there is still a website today dedicated to her memory. The darker the night, the brighter the star.

Are you living in the right place for you? What may have been fine when you were younger may now be too big, or not accessible for visiting your family. Maybe your friends have moved away and left you marooned.

## Friends

Are your friends going to support you in this new life or are you going to have to make some new ones? You may soon find you have left some of them behind, but in your new venture there will be new forward-looking friends to support and encourage you.

## Travel

Will travel be important in your next step?

Do any of these describe you?

*Adrenaline Junkie, Africa Fan, Backpacker, Beach Lover, Camper, Cruiser, European Geocacher, Hitchhiker, Lover of Asia, Mountaineer, Road Tripper, Sailor, Skier, Solo Traveller, South American Traveller, Travel Addict, US Lover*

**Hobbies**

Are your current hobbies going to blossom into a success story or are you going to branch out into some new fields?

*Antique Collecting, Boating, Calligraphy, Cooking, Crafts, Dancing, Embroidery, Gardening, Genealogy, Knitting, Languages, Painting, Playing an Instrument, Pottery, Quilting, Running, Sewing, Singing, Writing*

Look back at your journal notes so far and by now it should be clearer which parts of your life you would like to alter en route to success, which new fields you might investigate and which parts of your life are holding you up.

The next question is this: where are you actually going?

# Workbook Day 4

**Personality**

How are my relationships? (good/bad/indifferent)

Do I wish to change them? (Y/N)

If so, what do I have to do?

..................................................................................

..................................................................................

..................................................................................

..................................................................................

..................................................................................

..................................................................................

..................................................................................

..................................................................................

..................................................................................

..................................................................................

Does my next move (mental or physical) involve other people? (Y/N)

Does this present a challenge? (Y/N)

If so, how can I address this?

...........................................................................................

...........................................................................................

...........................................................................................

...........................................................................................

...........................................................................................

...........................................................................................

...........................................................................................

...........................................................................................

...........................................................................................

...........................................................................................

...........................................................................................

Am I looking for a partner? (Y/N)

Am I happy with my partner? (Y/N)

**Health**

Am I comfortable with my weight? (Y/N)

If not, how am I going to address this?

.......................................................................................................

.......................................................................................................

.......................................................................................................

.......................................................................................................

.......................................................................................................

.......................................................................................................

.......................................................................................................

.......................................................................................................

.......................................................................................................

.......................................................................................................

.......................................................................................................

Am I suffering from a limiting illness? (Y/N)

Do I have physical limitations? (Y/N)

Am I happy with my current level of exercise to keep me fit? (Y/N)

If not, what am I going to do about it?

.........................................................................................

.........................................................................................

.........................................................................................

.........................................................................................

.........................................................................................

.........................................................................................

## Finances

Are my finances in good shape? (Y/N)

If not, what do I have to do? (new job/cut expenses/move)

.........................................................................................

.........................................................................................

.........................................................................................

.........................................................................................

.........................................................................................

.........................................................................................

**My Home**

Am I happy in my home? (Y/N)

If not, what can I do about it?

..........................................................................................

..........................................................................................

..........................................................................................

..........................................................................................

..........................................................................................

..........................................................................................

How can I make this happen?

..........................................................................................

..........................................................................................

..........................................................................................

..........................................................................................

..........................................................................................

..........................................................................................

..........................................................................................

**Travel**

Is Travel important to me? (Y/N)

If so, am I a/an Adrenaline Junkie, Africa Fan, Backpacker, Beach Lover, Camper, Cruiser, European Geocacher, Hitchhiker, Lover of Asia, Mountaineer, Road Tripper, Sailor, Skier, Solo Traveller, South American Traveller, Travel Addict, US Lover?

How can I make travel happen?

........................................................................

........................................................................

........................................................................

........................................................................

........................................................................

........................................................................

........................................................................

........................................................................

........................................................................

........................................................................

**Hobbies**

Do I want to progress existing hobbies or take up new ones?

Antique Collecting, Boating, Calligraphy, Cooking, Crafts, Dancing, Embroidery, Gardening, Genealogy, Knitting, Languages, Painting, Playing an Instrument, Pottery, Quilting, Running, Sewing, Singing, Writing

Which hobbies do I want to choose or extend?

...........................................................................................

...........................................................................................

How can I make this happen?

...........................................................................................

...........................................................................................

...........................................................................................

...........................................................................................

...........................................................................................

...........................................................................................

...........................................................................................

**Day 5**

Where are you going? What does happiness/success look and feel like?

# Day 5

## Where are you going? What does happiness/ success look and feel like?

'Success is liking yourself, liking what you do and liking how you do it.' (Maya Angelou)[14]

'Every great dream begins with a dreamer. Always remember you have within you the strength, the patience and the passion to reach for the stars and change the world.' (Harriet Tubman)[15]

Harriet Tubman became famous as a 'conductor' on the Underground Railroad in the US during the turbulent

1850s. Born a slave on Maryland's Eastern Shore she endured the harsh existence of a field hand including brutal beatings. In 1849 she fled slavery and, despite a bounty on her head, she returned to the South at least nineteen times to lead her family and hundreds of other slaves to freedom. 'I freed a thousand slaves,' she said. 'I could have freed a thousand more if only they knew they were slaves.'

This is where things begin to get exciting.

The defined GOAL(S) should now be coming into focus. It is important to both write down and visualise exactly what your future success looks and feels like. Is it an Internet business that goes viral and you begin exporting your wares all over the world? Are you going to build a bookshelf? Is it a downsized house, furnished and decorated in your dream colour schemes? Is it a world cruise? Can you see the exotic sights of India, the coral reefs of Australia and the Maori of New Zealand? The things that have been holding you back have been identified and dealt with.

How far do you think you can go? Set the target a little further away than that. When you start using the toolkit this book provides, you will amaze yourself as you see just how far you can go.

'I did then what I knew how to do. Now that I know better I do better.' (Maya Angelou)[16]

It is a good idea to have a soft opening to your new approach to life. The people around you will be comfortable with who you are and how available you are. Things may change when you have a life of your own.

1.  Make a list of all the things you would like to do, from doing a university course to building a tiny house, from opening a coffee shop to having a massage. Make sure there are at least 10 items on it.

2.  Prioritise the items on the list and then concentrate on the first four.

3.  Work out what time you have available during the week to do or prepare for these amazing things.

4.  For each of these propositions for success work out what is stopping you from doing it. Is it time? Is it money? Is it lack of expertise? Is it lack of confidence? Is it your family commitments? Would a friend be able to help you achieve your goal?

5.  List the steps you need to take to overcome each hurdle.

6.  Give yourself a time limit for achieving each one.

For example: By September, I will have done a gardening course; by Christmas, I shall have completed my own gardening makeover; by April, I shall be running a successful gardening business.

Make a vision board with pictures of your new life, whether it is a new house, a new dog, a new business or a new project. Add inspirational sayings or beautiful pictures, anything that will uplift and inspire you.

Now you have a plan to achieve these goals SUCCESSFULLY!

# Workbook Day 5

List of things I want to do to make my life more successful:

1. ...................................................................

2. ...................................................................

3. ...................................................................

4. ...................................................................

5. ...................................................................

6. ...................................................................

7. ...................................................................

8. ...................................................................

9. ...................................................................

10. ..................................................................

Put one word by each signifying why you haven't done it yet e.g. time, family commitments, money, insufficient space, no materials, lack of expertise.

Prioritise the list

Rewrite the top four items on your list in order of priority.

1. ...............................................................

2. ...............................................................

3. ...............................................................

4. ...............................................................

Add the steps you need to take to overcome the hurdles (barrier breakers) and a time frame for completion.

**Game plan**

| Aims | Barrier Breakers | Time Frame |
|------|------------------|------------|
| Item 1 | | |
| Item 2 | | |

| Aims | Barrier Breakers | Time Frame |
|---|---|---|
| Item 3 | | |
| Item 4 | | |

Ideas for my vision board

**Day 6**

# Pulling together the plan

# Day 6

## Pulling together the plan

Bridget and I are delighted that you have got to this part of Success @ 60+. As a Superlifer you are now officially afloat and rafting down the river of change.

Next, we are tackling the white water of worry where you may feel tossed and uncertain. Hang on in there; there is calmer water ahead. You are now free to be excited by the possibilities of the future and the fact that you are ready to make the years ahead work for you, as you start over loosed from the ties that have bound you previously, either internally or externally.

Daily happiness practice will be changing from an exercise into a lifestyle. Adopt an exercise for a month and it becomes a habit. By now you are starting to prove that.

Here in Alderney, I asked Eileen, a remarkable lady well into her second decade of Superlife, about her tips for Superlife success. 'Never worry' was her prompt reply. 'I have delegated that to my husband – he does enough for both of us; it only wastes time.'

Eileen is an amazing woman. She has formed the Salvation Army Strippers, who knit strips instead of squares (in case you were wondering!), and she has made over 140 blankets this way as well as dresses and jumpers, all for the Tumaini Fund in Tanzania, which educates and cares for 10,000 AIDS orphans.

'I will help anyone I can and I am grateful for every day, whatever the weather. A heart attack eleven years ago put everything into perspective. If something is difficult, tackle it the best way you can.' The Tumaini Fund founder Dr Susan Wilson MBE is herself an inspirational lady: www.tumainifund.org.uk.

Doing things for others gives enormous satisfaction and pleasure but if there is a gnawing void of unhappiness within you, you need to fill it with love before you go any further. Perhaps you have neglected yourself for many years and filled your time with displacement activities for family and friends. If that is the case, every morning sit still for a moment, shut your eyes and imagine your heart as a dried up leathery old wreck, which you drop into a bowl of clear sparkling water. As the water is absorbed it begins to swell and grow and becomes young and beautiful again. These are interesting words, implying that beauty is the prerogative of the young. Yet there is a beauty in the Superlifer that can only come with age. It is a beauty of spirit. Our society is obsessed with the external, which fades with age. Our boobs may have dropped, we may have a frog throat, our waists may have disappeared into the mists of time, but there can be a beauty in our eyes, in our words, in our being.

The power of our thoughts is transmitted to others, so if you are constantly worrying about the externals people will pick up on that. If you are concentrating on your success project, passionate in what you are doing and excited about the future, you will have the Superlife look, which is not the same as the young look but powerfully attractive.

If we are always trying to be something we are not, it is a disaster. You need only look at older women who have had facelifts to see they are often not worth the money. A facelift cannot remove discontentment. We need to adopt a style that is not aping or deferring to the young; a Superlifer look that says, yes I am who I am and proud of it. When you do your hair in the morning, look in the mirror, gaze into your eyes and be proud of what you see there.

You have so much to give, both to yourself and to the world. Success will enable you to stand tall and look the world in the eye, no longer slouched and emitting negativity. Standing tall will help you to breathe more deeply and get more oxygen into your body, enabling important changes on every level.

Ruth Hughes, a fashion designer living in Alderney, has these tips for the authentic Superlifer look.

1. Find your own style and stick to it; don't follow fashion slavishly.

2. Choose clothes that are 'body-skimming'. Tight clothes expose the bumps and lumps we would prefer to keep to ourselves. Our garments should leave a little to the imagination but follow the body contours. The Mary Portas collection ticks all the boxes.

3. Wear long tops with black tights or leggings if your legs are your best feature (unless you have cellulite). If those legs are really worth exposure, go for the short skirt.

4. Avoid beige at all costs. If you are determined to go with beige, for goodness sake enliven with a little colour!

5. Try the ethnic look with a kaftan, for example, for a cool summer change. They're also great for nightwear when travelling. If you need to face the world unexpectedly you are then ready for anything.

6. Hair can make or break a look. A good cut is worth its weight in gold. Dyed hair can make you look as though you are sporting a helmet. Go grey gracefully, but if you need a little colour go for highlights.

7.  Always remember to check how you look from the rear!

8.  Shoes need to be comfortable and sandals will often accommodate the bunion brigade. Pumps and wedges look good for those who can wear them.

9.  Look at your body and decide which are the best bits and accentuate them with what you wear. If you have slim hips don't cover them up with a baggy top; if you have a large bust don't let a top hang straight from your boobs as it will make what's below look bigger.

10. A bad posture will ruin any outfit.

Carmen Dell'Orefice is still a supermodel at eighty-two. Her take is this: 'We are all works of art in progress.'[17]

Marjorie, into her second Superlife decade, stands out to me as particularly smart. Always immaculately turned out, she says, 'My mother taught me always to look my best. Perfect make-up is essential as is your hairstyle and colour. I know what looks good and I stick to that. Your attitude to life is crucial; make the best of every day, glass half-full, never half-empty.'

How do you get rid of the worry and anxiety that creeps in and blights your best efforts, you may ask? Worry is a habit along with happiness. Of course you can choose to worry but worry also tends to creep up when you least expect it and before you know it, it has its feet under the table and has taken over your mind. It is one of those habits that eats away at your energy and must be stopped in its tracks.

What exactly is worry?

In worry mode your mind is in a closed loop of 'what if' thoughts. What goes on in your head is a result of chemicals, which in turn are secreted into your body as a result of the thought processes. A common example is the presence of a lion in close proximity, which prompts the adrenaline rush that enables you to run away quickly.

The worry chemical effect was clearly demonstrated the other night when my husband, who is a diabetic, had a severe hypoglycaemic attack. This means that his blood glucose fell to abnormally low levels. He suddenly became obsessively frightened and worried. Eight glucose tablets later he was OK.

There are no tablets to reverse worry (unless you go for antidepressants) but as you are now in control, you can stop the thoughts that lead to the closed circuit.

Worry has no place in your new life and your new habits will stop worry in its tracks. This is very important, as you need every ounce of energy to make the positive happen. If you wake up with a cloud over your head every morning, which is there before you even open your eyes, think about what you did the night before.

Depending on the programme, watching television just before you turn in may banish sleep and encourage worry to be your bedfellow. There is a very powerful time as you pass from wakefulness to sleep. Put the vision board you made yesterday by the bed to remind you where you are headed. I have used inspirational music to send me to sleep if my mind is overactive. Concentrating on your breath, counting it in and counting it out, is so boring you will fall asleep in no time and worry can't get a foot in the door.

I am a great fan of meditation. I ended up with a wonky heart whilst looking after the oldies and the doctors wanted to put me on tablets. I promised to come back in three months for review having 1) reduced my workload, 2) begun sitting down daily for half an hour (with Bridget), and 3) started practising daily meditation. Three months later my heart had returned to normal without chemical intervention.

I recommend *Silence Your Mind* by Dr Ramesh Manocha.[18]

If meditation is not your scene then get one of the wonderful adult colouring books currently on the market. Emma Farrarons' *Mindfulness Colouring Book* is my favourite.[19] Let filling in the detail take the place of nagging worry. Do it with your grandchildren!

Start the day as you mean to go on… as soon as you wake up start thanking somebody for something, building a barrier that worry can't penetrate. If you have no ideas, thank God for the day, the universe for the chance of a lifetime and Bridget and me for the book!

*Bridget comments ... We have mentioned having a good friend with whom to share these steps. Jane and I have been friends for over thirty-five years. Initially we had a lot in common through pre-school and small children but then we drifted apart as our lives changed.*

*Over the last ten years we have re-established that contact with mutual support and respect, which adds value to our lives. 'True friends are like bras, close to your heart and there for support!'*

*We truly are different though – meditation makes me edgy and uncomfortable but a good walk, in either the country, the town or by the sea, helps me set my thoughts in order and decide the next step.*

*I have also been interested recently in how many people I know, not geeks or weirdoes, who have pretty much stopped watching television. Some say it is all rubbish and some had found they were using it as mindless chatter for 'company' in the background. I am not against television per se but would recommend choosing what to watch and turning it off again after the programme!*

Book recommendation: *How To Stop Worrying and Start Living* by Simeon Lindstrom[20]

As I have mentioned, your nearest and dearest may take a little time to adjust to the new you and changing other people is not an option. Accept them and work around them (women are masters of truth economy) or ditch them. As suggested in the last chapter keep a sharp lookout for those who drain you. If you can help someone, then great but if they are a black hole they will swallow you whole and you will disappear without trace.

Happiness can be found in making a difference to other people's lives by inspiring them through your actions, whether this means baking cakes, making someone smile or motivating them to paint a masterpiece – so disappearing without trace does not cut the mustard. The black hole will not feel any happier and will wander off to find another victim to bleed dry.

Health is of prime importance; you need to be as well as you possibly can be to take on the challenges of success. Your health may limit your choices but as a result of reading this book you may find:

**ONE**

You can improve your health. Warning: at this stage your enthusiasm may inadvertently set you back a step or two.

Having read *Born to Run* by Christopher McDougall,[21] the amazing story of the Tarahumara Indians of Mexico who run barefoot all their lives from the cradle to the grave, I was inspired to take up running to improve my general fitness. Anyone can do it if they apply themselves, I figured. I have never ever run, not even in my youth, but was frustrated that I was being outrun on the cricket field by my grandchildren.

I have always enjoyed going barefoot so I would steal out when no one was looking and run round a nearby field. The result: a damaged Achilles tendon. For those who don't know, it is a horrible condition that means all I can do is stagger.

Far from becoming the super-athlete of my dreams I feel older than my years and have begun to put on weight as I can't even exercise the dogs! To put a positive spin on it, it has enabled me to sit down and write this book while I wait for my body to heal. The moral of this tale is DON'T rush things and if in doubt consult a fitness expert!

*Bridget comments … I knew Jane was mad – running for a bus is my limit and only then if it's the last bus. Ten months ago I had both hips replaced in separate operations one month apart and spent a total of sixteen weeks on crutches. Now, six months later, I no longer use a car on the island and walk anywhere I need to go without giving it a second thought. (Alderney is only three miles by one mile though!) This week I am back on my beloved bike; just a couple of short rides completed so far, but I'm getting there and thoroughly enjoying the journey.*

## TWO

You can work around your health restrictions. With one leg all strapped at least I can practise some yoga/Pilates postures and get some of my muscles toned.

## THREE

You could look seriously at some complementary therapies such as homeopathy, acupuncture, Pilates, yoga and the Bowen technique, all of which treat the person rather than the condition. Google any of the above therapies to find your local properly qualified practitioner. For example, if you would like to try Pilates, visit www.pilatesnearyou.co.uk. Helena Belither, based in London, provides both classes and individual tuition, if you would prefer not to be in a group situation: www.pilatesbyhelena.co.uk. 'Pilates is especially suitable for the 60+ age group as it is a low impact form of exercise designed to not only improve core strength but also improve your wellbeing. If you are suffering from an injury or poor health Pilates can help restore physical vitality, invigorate the mind and elevate the spirit.'[22]

Many chemical solutions contain, rather than cure, a medical condition. Taking a cocktail of chemical medicines over a lifetime can in some circumstances cause serious problems for the human body. The pharmaceutical companies can't do trials over a lifetime; the drug would never get to market. In acute illness chemistry can be lifesaving, but adverse drug reactions (ADRs) are one of the leading causes of death, according to the US Food and Drug Administration (FDA).[23]

I am not averse to chemical solutions per se. They keep my husband alive – he would be dead in three days if his insulin were not available – but it is worth taking time to check out what your medication is doing/has done to your body.

Also check out Jason Vale's video 'Super Juice Me!',[24] a very thought-provoking documentary about our diets, our relationship with medicine and drugs and the use of juiced fruit in chronic conditions. However, NEVER change your medication without first consulting your doctor.

*Bridget comments ... Forget the chronic conditions – some of the juices and smoothies are just amazing. My favourite treat is no longer chocolate but a banana, yoghurt and cinnamon smoothie; it is not only heavenly but does you a power of good too!*

**FOUR**

You could look online for comprehensive information on the physical effects of aging and the way in which vitamins can profoundly influence a number of health issues. I tend to use a company called Healthspan to guide me through this minefield of information: www.healthspan.co.uk.

If you use health as a reason for not carrying out your Superlife plan you are selling yourself short. If you have low energy, do one baby step a day. Assess where you are and what you can change.

All through this book we are challenging assumptions. Is your health really stuck where you think it is or is there something you can do? Your body is a wonderfully complex series of chemical reactions, constantly repairing itself. If there is a chronic condition the body may decide of its own volition to relegate the repair to the 'later or never' column.

Complementary therapies such as acupuncture can often gently reactivate the repair process, move the obstacles and let the body continue its incredible work.

Listen to your body and see how it reacts to different foods. If you have time and can do a timed food diary, write down what and when you eat and check how you feel after each meal. What slows you down and what speeds you up? What wakes you up and what sends you to sleep?

I keep going on about energy but it is the key to giving yourself the 'get up and go' you will need to effect these changes. Vitamins may be helpful here. How far you want to go down the diet modification route depends on how important it is to you. As a society we have gone overboard on proteins and dairy produce. No other animal group drinks milk all their lives. Cows' milk is a product for baby cows, not adult humans or even adult cows.

I find that the more vegetables and fruit I have in my diet, the lighter and more alive I feel. I have recently got rid of caffeine in my diet, which has taken my headaches with it, and replaced it with juicing. A juice in the morning is the equivalent for me of a stimulant. It looks so beautiful and tastes divine and gives me a boot up the backside. People moan about cleaning their juicers. I timed my wash-up the other day; it was three minutes. I rest my case.

I also have a NutriBullet®,[25] which makes the most delicious smoothies. It is excellent because my grandchildren can easily and safely make their own. The result is not as concentrated as a juice but you do get the fibre that is otherwise wasted. I also discovered the machine is a lifesaver when your pancake batter goes lumpy or you want to make your own Baileys-style cream liqueur. Yes, I do have some vices!

Juicing and smoothies are wonderful when I am busy. They take two to three minutes to make and give you all the nutrients you need in a flash. I am not a dietician but when I discovered that ultra runners who push their bodies to incredible extremes can do it on a plant power diet, I realised how far we have come from what is healthy for us.

Additionally, these extreme runners' bodies constantly have a heavy repair schedule as their muscles get damaged by hours running on the tracks and trails so their diets need to be perfect to support them.

Fluids are very important for all our bodily functions as well as hydrating our skin and reducing our wrinkles.

Drinking two litres a day is good, as the human body at our age is about fifty per cent water. Our blood is eighty per cent water, our brain is eighty to eighty-five per cent water, our lungs are seventy-five to eighty per cent water, our liver is seventy to seventy-five per cent water, our skin is seventy per cent water, our kidneys are eighty to eighty-five per cent water, our muscles are seventy to seventy-five per cent water, our heart is seventy-five to eighty per cent water and our bones are twenty to twenty-five per cent water, so if you want your body to work well, keep drinking![26]

Excess weight is something that is often a problem – both real and perceived – but so much has been written about it that I'm not going to add any more. You will find what works for you. We all have different metabolisms and different foods affect people in different ways.

If you are finding weight hard to shift, look at what medications you are taking and list them. Often you will find weight that clings like a limpet is a side effect of the tablets you have been prescribed.

The Jason Vale books and app on juicing/smoothies are excellent. He has used juices to deal with a large number of long-standing serious medical conditions with great results. I find his weight loss juice diet excellent. With juices every three hours for five to seven days you never have time to feel hungry.

*Bridget comments ... I get really stuck trying to do a 'just juice' diet, so I have one in the morning and a salad lunch, to which I add fruit, nuts, various herbs and sometimes cheese. I nibble on chilled celery or apples and have a banana smoothie at night. I'm not slim, I am overweight but I am getting there – I'm not even aiming to be slim but to be feeling great. I get one cheat day a week for a lunch with friends. And, let's be honest, the occasional cheat just because…!*

Books I would recommend:

*The Plantpower Way* by Rich Roll and Julie Piat[27]

*The 4-Hour Body* by Timothy Ferriss[28] (a totally different take on weight loss that definitely challenges assumptions)

*Deliciously Ella* by Ella Woodward[29] (a great cookbook if you think your problems are gut-related)

*The Juice Master Diet: 7lbs in 7 days* by Jason Vale[30]

*The Juice Master: Turbo-charge your life in 14 days* by Jason Vale[31]

Websites I would recommend:

www.healthspan.co.uk

Equipment I would recommend:

A juicer and a NutriBullet® for smoothies

We get energy from our food and from our happiness but where are the hidden drains on it? Do you have leaks in your system?

1. There may be an underlying medical problem that has not been tackled. It is always wise to have a blood test if you are persistently tired for no reason or have any other unexplained symptoms or changes in your health.

2. The people known as black holes can drain you emotionally.

3. If you live constantly in work overload mode, you'll be carrying an energy-sapping 'To Be Done' (TBD) list in your head that never gets finished.

4. Baggage from the past that you are carrying around with you, particularly guilt, drains your energy. Emotional Freedom Technique (EFT) is wonderful for sorting that out. It enables you to pinpoint baggage problems quickly and accurately (you may have spent sixty plus years with inaccurate suppositions) and to sort them out immediately.

5. Gary Craig (founder of EFT but not a medical practitioner) explains: 'EFT is a universal healing tool that can provide impressive results for physical, emotional and performance issues. EFT operates on the premise that no matter what part of your life needs improvement, there are unresolved

emotional issues in the way. Even for physical issues, chronic pain, or diagnosed conditions, it is common knowledge that any kind of emotional stress can impede the natural healing potential of the human body.'[32] Are you sleeping badly? This can be due to many factors including worry (already tackled), medication, a poor mattress or a sleeping partner who thrashes around. I solved that particular problem by pushing two single beds together, lashing them so they couldn't separate and putting on a mattress topper.

Just a word about your TBD list: carrying round jobs in your head is a great energy drain so commit them to paper and leave them there. Each night take a sheet with four columns and head them Tomorrow, Next Week, Outsource and Never.

See how many jobs you can put in the 'Never' column! It is also surprising how many jobs someone else could do if you asked them or paid them! (How much is your time worth?)

Label tasks 'Mission Critical' that are crucial to your success project, or 'Mundane' if they are important but don't add value, like ironing.

The timing of tasks is critical. You may find dividing up the day into slots is helpful.

6.00-8.00 Owls get nothing done; extra Mission Critical tasks for larks

8.00-9.00 Mundane tasks and email checking; try not to be distracted by Facebook

9.00-12.00 Mission Critical tasks

12.00-13.00 Lunch, exercise and Mundane tasks

13.00-16.00 Mission Critical tasks

16.00-17.00 Mundane tasks and email checking; the more Mundane tasks you get done in the morning the sooner you can be off the hook now

21.00-23.00 Larks get nothing done; extra Mission Critical tasks for owls

You may need to hide from the world or your partner during Mission Critical periods to enable solid work to be done. If Mission Critical times are not exciting then you are not doing what you really want to do, so change your goals.

*Bridget comments ... We did say we were different and this is a good example. Unlike Jane, I choose to approach every day differently. However, I DO use lists and, like Jane, believe lists are essential for clearing the clutter in my mind.*

*Some things crop up regularly and obviously, like ironing and mowing. Depending on your circumstances, some things are daily tasks but still take a bit of time. These should ideally slot into the*

*same place each day and become so automatic that you don't list them.*

*My failing tends to be planning more than is reasonable for each section of my day. But I always try to fit in a sensible amount so I can go to bed with a sense of achievement and not exhaustion.*

*So make the lists; put a couple of things into the 'if I have time' section, then do your best each day – but don't beat yourself up. If a friend phones or drops in for coffee, remember that they are WAY more important to you, and you to them, than mowing, ironing, painting or whatever else is on your list. Relax and enjoy them – and reshuffle the list if you must.*

Parkinson's Law
'A task will swell in proportion to the amount of time you give yourself to complete it.'

Your time perception of a task may also be unrealistic. You may put something off for days and when you get down to it, it only takes fifteen minutes. But for all that time it has been draining your energy. Assuming you will never get everything done is unfortunately a self-fulfilling prophecy.

**Key point:** Being busy is not being successful. Pareto's law states that eighty per cent of the results of an activity are produced by twenty per cent of the effort, so look carefully where your results are coming from and concentrate your precious energies there.

The ability to create time is a combination of planning and focus.

Plan and batch your mundane tasks to once a week:

Batch your shopping
Batch your cookery
Batch your ironing
Batch your gardening

Stick to whatever schedule you have chosen and keep a picture of your goal in the loo, over the sink, by your bed, by the computer and anywhere else you spend time so you never lose sight of it, whatever the distractions.

Downsizing may be an option at this time of life when the old birds and the fledglings have finally flown the nest. Do you really want to spend your life on domestic and gardening duties if your heart lies elsewhere? With pensions not being brilliant, the capital difference a house sale may release could come in handy. To buy a house with lots of steps and a sloping garden may not be the best idea at your age, but everyone has their preferences. Just bear in mind that mobility may be an issue at some point and at that stage you may not want or be able to move house again.

Bridget is selling up and going nomadic which is another option.

*Bridget comments ... I was fortunate enough to meet my husband just before my twenty-first birthday. He already had two teenage sons. Two more children, seven grandchildren and three great-grandchildren later, John died when I was sixty after a short stay in hospital and a long illness that we managed together at home.*

*I looked at my wonderful, busy life filled on a daily basis with friends and family and thought, 'is that it?'*

*I am in the process of downsizing, which is cathartic in itself – a mixture of tears and laughter. I'm putting my truly precious bits in store, selling my house, leaving my island home and going to 'see what is out there'. That is literally my plan – I have a few tentative ideas, but when people ask, 'Where are you going? What will you do?' I can honestly say, 'I don't know.'*

*It's terrifying, it's exciting and eventually I will 'know', but in the meantime I am enjoying the process, enjoying the journey.*

*Jane adds … My grandchildren are in Cornwall so my next project after downsizing is to make or buy a tiny home on a trailer so I can stay without disrupting the various households. The YouTube videos on tiny houses are fascinating and at www.tinyhouseuk.co.uk they can create one for you, at whatever level you desire, from flat pack to completion.*

*What interested me is that people who downsize to a tiny home do so because they don't want to spend*

*their time maintaining real estate. I am not sure that*
*accessing the bed by a ladder is the most sensible thing*
*at our stage but there are ways around that.*

Downsizing means decluttering. Success @ 60+ depends on targeting your goal and focusing all your energies in that direction. We have talked about decluttering the mind from worry and other distractions, but now we turn to decluttering your physical environment, literally putting your house in order, even if you are not downsizing.

Interestingly, Marie Kondo in *The Life-Changing Magic of Tidying*[33] explains that the success of tidying lies in the mind. 'Success is ninety per cent dependent on our mindset [...] if we do not address this aspect, rebound is inevitable no matter how much is discarded or how cleverly things are organised.' Her mantra is 'do it in one go' and your mindset will change.

'When people return to clutter no matter how much they tidy, it is not their room or their belongings but their way of thinking that is at fault.' Clear the clutter in your house and you can sort the clutter in your mind, which may have been instrumental in preventing you from achieving the sort of success for which you are striving.

'Although not large, the space I live in is graced only with the things that speak to my heart. My lifestyle brings me joy,' says Marie Kondo. Don't focus on what you need to discard, but on cherishing the things you want to keep. It's the same old story – place your focus on the positive not the negative.

*Bridget comments ... I've always thought of decluttering as a 'do it in one go' exercise and several times over the forty years of family life, we've moved or I've got the declutter bug.*

*Last year, while confined to crutches and immobile, my sister came to stay and I decided to declutter a bookcase – a BIG bookcase. Almost two hundred books later, the shelves had space for an ornament or two and a couple of photographs and I was 'done'.*

*Now that my move is organised I am looking at the packing and the 'essential' books I had kept. Well, another fifty or so will bless the RNLI charity shop this weekend. It is the same with the pots and pans and the music – I no longer have a child learning piano and if I did, one tutor book would suffice.*

*Decluttering to me is a continual and pleasurable activity – never finite. Our choices change and something that was essential six months ago may just be clutter today. Don't feel you have to get rid of it now just because you are decluttering and it's clearly clutter but YOUR clutter. One day you will let it go with joy and relief and that day it will truly be clutter.*

## Finance

'Money is the root of all evil.' Not so; it is the LOVE of money that is the root of all evil. It is clearly wrong when money becomes an obsession. Money is a tool, not an end in itself. It enables you to do things either for yourself or others. Concentrate on abundance, however red the bank balance looks; if you think poor you will attract poverty.

> *Bridget comments ... There is a great truth in the old adage of 'take care of the pennies and the pounds will take care of themselves.' I've always found knowing where I stood financially easier to cope with than guessing.*
>
> *If it was really dire, and there have been times, I would focus on how NOT to spend rather than on how to earn what I hadn't got. Do I really need that? If I ate this instead, I'd spend less. (An apple instead of a doughnut makes sense on all levels.)*
>
> *As a stepping-stone to success there is no menial job I wouldn't tackle if I needed to. Pride comes from fending for oneself, whether that means washing up, sweeping streets or doing a paper round. Pride in doing it well is what matters.*

As a final thought it is good to look at your reactions to certain situations. For example, might your reaction to money be unhelpful or outmoded, and can you now discard this in the light of experience?

If a dog barks at you and you feel frightened, every time that situation occurs, you will experience the same response. This is because your brain has a complex monitoring system that automatically checks up what happened in similar situations and responds accordingly. You are now frightened of dogs and a victim of circumstance. A vicious cycle has developed.

If you want to break into the happiness/success cycle, all you have to do is ask WHY? You might reply,

'I don't know.'

'Well, guess', I say.

Then it slowly comes to you, because only YOU can answer that question. 'Oh yes, I remember I got bitten by a dog when I was very small.'

The adult reply is, 'Does that mean all dogs are biters?'

'No, and I probably did something as a small child to provoke that response. So I don't need that automatic response when I see dogs now; I can swap it for a more rational approach.'

The WHY question is invaluable, particularly when the answer on the surface might seem obvious. Drill down to find why you are dissatisfied/unhappy in certain circumstances or situations and which parts of your life need re-surfacing; but do it gently and with love.

# Workbook Day 6

Do I need to address my wardrobe? (Y/N)

Is there a predominant colour? (Y/N)

If so, what is it?

...................................................................................

Is that intentional or habit? (Y/N)

Does it suit me? (Y?N)

If no, what colours could I try?

...................................................................................

...................................................................................

...................................................................................

Which type of clothes do I prefer?
(dresses/trousers/skirts)

Is that right for me now? (Y/N)

What type of clothes would I like in my wardrobe?

..................................................................................................

..................................................................................................

..................................................................................................

..................................................................................................

..................................................................................................

..................................................................................................

..................................................................................................

..................................................................................................

What shoes do I have?

..................................................................................................

..................................................................................................

..................................................................................................

..................................................................................................

..................................................................................................

..................................................................................................

..................................................................................................

What type of shoes suit me?

Heel ...........................................................................

Shape ...........................................................................

Colour ...........................................................................

Do I have suitable accessories that match my style?
(Y/N)

If no, what do I need?

...........................................................................

...........................................................................

...........................................................................

...........................................................................

...........................................................................

...........................................................................

...........................................................................

...........................................................................

...........................................................................

...........................................................................

Based on results of the above questions what do I need to recycle?

1. ................................................................

2. ................................................................

3. ................................................................

4. ................................................................

5. ................................................................

6. ................................................................

7. ................................................................

8. ................................................................

9. ................................................................

10. ................................................................

Do I need to restyle my hair? (Y/N)

If so, what style shall I choose?

.........................................................................................

.........................................................................................

**24-hour food diary**

| Date/Time | Food/Drink | Effect |
|-----------|-----------|--------|
|           |           |        |

Do I need to look at my diet? (Y/N)

If so, what steps am I going to take?

..............................................................................................

..............................................................................................

..............................................................................................

..............................................................................................

..............................................................................................

..............................................................................................

..............................................................................................

..............................................................................................

..............................................................................................

..............................................................................................

Am I remembering to drink enough water? (Y/N)

If not, what am I going to do about it?

..............................................................................................

..............................................................................................

..............................................................................................

Do I need to look at my caffeine intake? (Y/N)

If so, how am I going to manage it?

..............................................................................................

..............................................................................................

..............................................................................................


Are all the tablets I take really necessary? (Y/N)

List your tablets and reasons for taking them, but
ALWAYS consult your doctor before changing your
medication regime.

..............................................................................................

..............................................................................................

..............................................................................................

..............................................................................................

..............................................................................................

..............................................................................................

..............................................................................................

..............................................................................................

..............................................................................................

Energy leaks

1. .......................................................

2. .......................................................

3. .......................................................

4. .......................................................

5. .......................................................

6. .......................................................

**To Be Done List**

Mark each job Mission Critical to success or Mundane. (Try and outsource the Mundane ones!)

| Tomorrow | Next Week | Outsource | Never |
| --- | --- | --- | --- |
| | | | |

## Job Schedule

6.00-8.00 extra time for larks

..........................................................................................................

8.00-9.00

..........................................................................................................

9.00-12.00

..........................................................................................................

12.00-13.00

..........................................................................................................

13.00-16.00

..........................................................................................................

16.00-17.00

..........................................................................................................

21.00-23.00 extra time for owls

..........................................................................................................

Do I need to declutter? (Y/N)

If yes, which items are cluttering my life at the moment?

.................................................................................................

.................................................................................................

.................................................................................................

.................................................................................................

.................................................................................................

.................................................................................................

.................................................................................................

.................................................................................................

Who could benefit from my preloved items?

.................................................................................................

.................................................................................................

.................................................................................................

.................................................................................................

.................................................................................................

.................................................................................................

.................................................................................................

Which items could be sold to boost my finances?

.................................................................................................

.................................................................................................

.................................................................................................

.................................................................................................

.................................................................................................

.................................................................................................

.................................................................................................

.................................................................................................

I am proud to say that these are the first results of taking my Superlife in both hands and running with it. When I look back in a year I shall be amazed how far I have come!

# Day 7

# Conclusion

# Day 7

## Conclusion

As I write this, my eyes drift across the rooftops to the ocean. Their scaly backs are bathed in the rosy glow of a perfectly still June morning against a backdrop of sea as still as a millpond and a misty horizon heralding the scorcher of a day to come. The collared doves celebrate this incredible beauty by calling to each other from the branches of our flowering cherry tree.

Jonathan Livingston Seagull glides past, picking up an invisible thermal and disappearing in the direction of France. He has broken the boundaries of convention, of other seagulls' expectations: he has found a meaning to life. 'It's true! I am a perfect unlimited gull,' he says to Chiang the Elder. Later, after he has taught the lessons he has learned to others, he explains to his newest class, who complain they can't do what he and his older students are doing, 'The only difference, the very only one is that they have begun to understand what they really are and have begun to practise it.'

Now you understand what you really are; go out and practise.

Read *Jonathan Livingston Seagull* by Richard Bach[34]

The presence of a greater power is palpable in this silence of early morning mist, before the heat and noise of the day. For me as a Christian it is the divine, but others will see it in different ways. To connect with the spiritual side of our beings lifts us to another level and it fast tracks us to be what we were created to be, beautiful, free and pushing the boundaries of success, whatever age we are.

If we can inspire each other to make our dreams a living reality, when this book is widely read there will be a chain reaction on a global scale sufficient to change the world.

You are now part of that chain which is indisputably awesome and we are so proud of you. Our next book will be YOUR story to inspire others.

Send it to us NOW: success60plus@gmail.com!

I would like the Iron Nun to have the final word.

'To serve the world around you, give the world what you have, and serve the world with what you are.'[35]

What better reason could there be for success?

# Bibliography

[1] Kaufman Barry Neil *Happiness is a Choice* Fawcett Columbine, Ballantine Books 1991, Kaufman Barry Neil *Power Dialogues* Epic Century Publishers 2000/2001

[2] Kaufman Raun *Autism Breakthrough* St Martin's Press 2014

[3] Buder Sister Madonna *The Grace to Race* Simon & Schuster 2010

[4] Dalai Lama http://www.brainyquote.com/quotes/quotes/d/dalailama166116.html

[5] Tara Darby/Robin Arzon http://www.runitout.co.uk/ http://www.robinarzon.com/

[6] Like the Wind Magazine www.likethewindmagazine.com

[7] Oprah Winfrey https://www.goodreads.com/quotes/470314-i-was-once-afraid-of-people-saying-who-does-she

[8] Gloria Steinem http://www.goodreads.com/quotes/11090-the-truth-will-set-you-free-but-first-it-will

[9] Maya Angelou http://www.goodreads.com/quotes/7980-i-can-be-changed-by-what-happens-to-me-but

[10] Quinn Lydia *21 Online Business Ideas You Can Start Tomorrow with No Money* Kindle

[11] Anne Wilson Schaef http://www.brainyquote.com/quotes/quotes/a/annewilson169935.html

[12] Myles Eckert https://armyhistory.org/foundation-thanks-myles-eckert-a-gold-star-kid/

[13] Peace Pilgrim www.peacepilgrim.com/

[14] Maya Angelou http://www.goodreads.com/quotes/1208-success-is-liking-yourself-liking-what-you-do-and-liking

[15] Harriet Tubman http://www.goodreads.com/quotes/5935-every-great-dream-begins-with-a-dreamer-always-remember-you

[16] Maya Angelou http://www.goodreads.com/quotes/9821-i-did-then-what-i-knew-how-to-do-now

[17] Carmen Dell'Orefice http://www.huffingtonpost.com/2014/02/06/carmen-dellorefice-model_n_4733401.html

[18] Dr Manocha Ramesh *Silence Your Mind* Hachette Australia 2013

[19] Farrarons Emma *Mindfulness Colouring Book* Boxtree Ltd 2015

[20] Lindstrom Simeon *How To Stop Worrying and Start Living* Kindle 2014

[21] McDougall Christopher *Born to Run* Random House 2009

[22] https://www.pilatesnearyou.co.uk/pilates_classes_benefits.php

[23] http://www.fda.gov/Drugs/DevelopmentApprovalProcess/
DevelopmentResources/DrugInteractionsLabeling/ucm114848.htm

[24] Vale Jason *Super Juice Me!* http://www.imdb.com/title/tt3529920/

[25] https://www.nutribullet.com/

[26] Distribution of water in the human body
http://www.Meandmybody.com

[27] Roll Rich *The Plantpower Way* Avery, Penguin Random House,
New York 2015

[28] Ferriss Timothy *The 4-Hour Body* Crown Publishing Group,
Random House Inc. NY 2010

[29] Woodward Ella *Deliciously Ella* Scribner 2015

[30] Vale Jason *The Juice Master Diet: 7lbs in 7 days* Harper Collins
2012

[31] Vale Jason *The Juice Master: Turbo-charge your life in 14 days*
Harper Collins 2010

[32] EFT http://www.emofree.com/

[33] Kondo Marie *The Life-Changing Magic of Tidying* Ten Speed Press Berkley 2014

[34] Bach Richard *Jonathan Livingston Seagull: The Complete Edition* Thorsons Classics 2015

[35] http://thisgivesmehope.com/2013/03/30/622-sister-madonna-buder-still-competing-in-her-80s/

Printed in Great Britain
by Amazon